OVERCOMING
TEMPTATION

DAMIAN KYLE

CALVARY CHAPEL PUBLISHING

SANTA ANA, CALIFORNIA

CONTENTS

FOREWORD

Several years ago, Damian Kyle was inspired to deliver a message from God's Word, which is as timeless as God's Word. I was privileged to hear that message, now contained in *Overcoming Temptation*.

Satan uses every means available to him to thwart God's purpose in our lives: Immorality and lust are just two examples of the sins of the mind and flesh that Satan uses to entrap God's people and foil God's plans.

This book exposes these devices with truth, God-given insight, and common sense. Damian outlines the progression of temptation and sets forth the path to gaining victory over sin.

By showing us how to obey God's command to "flee temptation," this message shines the beacon of truth on the path of escape.

Louis Neely
Warehouse Christian Ministries
Sacramento, California

With deep appreciation for their teaching and example,

this book is dedicated to

Chuck Smith, Gayle Erwin, and Bill MacDonald.

INTRODUCTION

Blessed is the man who endures temptation; for when he has been approved, he will receive the crown of life which the Lord has promised to those who love Him. Let no one say when he is tempted, "I am tempted by God"; for God cannot be tempted by evil, nor does He Himself tempt anyone. But each one is tempted when he is drawn away by his own desires and enticed. Then, when desire has conceived, it gives birth to sin; and sin, when it is full-grown, brings forth death. Do not be deceived, my beloved brethren.

James 1:12–16

WHAT IS TEMPTATION?

The subject of temptation ought to be of great interest to all believers. Every day, we are either facing temptations, coming through them, or about to encounter them. So the issue is not *whether* we are going to be tempted, but rather: Will we handle temptation properly *when* it comes?

James 1:12 tells us that *temptation to sin* is not sin. As Christians, we often put ourselves under a great deal of condemnation over the fact that we are tempted to do wrong. We think, "If I were a good Christian, if I were truly spiritual, I would be above temptation." But even Jesus was tempted by the Devil; yet without sin. In verse 13, James says, "Let no one say *when* he is tempted . . ." (emphasis mine).

God warns us that we will *all* be enticed by sin. We can, however, respond to temptation in such a way that it does not have to *lead to sin*. Temptation becomes sin when it is allowed to unite with our sinful desires (verse 14). Verse 15 tells us it is at that point that sin is "conceived." The word "conceived" means "to receive together." It is the word used to describe human reproduction. When the seed from the man is united with the egg from the woman, conception takes place. In the same way, temptation becomes sin when we allow it to unite with our sinful desires.

Imagine holding your left hand open in front of you—that open hand representing your will—then make a fist of your right hand, representing temptation. If you drive your fist into your open hand and the open hand refuses to embrace the fist, there is no conception because the two have not united. In the same way, when temptation hits your will and your will does not unite with it, then temptation has been properly handled. It does not become sin. But if that fist of temptation hits the open hand of your will and your open hand closes around the fist—your will no longer resisting it but now united with its intent—at that moment, sin has been conceived. The battle is won or lost in the realm of the will long before sin begins to be expressed outwardly. It begins when we allow ourselves to entertain thoughts about the pleasure of sin. That is why Solomon wrote, "The backslider *in heart* will be filled with his own ways" (Proverbs 14:14a, emphasis mine). Backsliding always begins in the heart, or the realm of the will.

Chapter One

JOSEPH: A MODEL OF SUCCESS

Now Joseph had been taken down to Egypt. And Potiphar, an officer of Pharaoh, captain of the guard, an Egyptian, bought him from the Ishmaelites who had taken him down there. The LORD was with Joseph, and he was a successful man; and he was in the house of his master the Egyptian. And his master saw that the LORD was with him and that the LORD made all he did to prosper in his hand. So Joseph found favor in his sight, and served him. Then he made him overseer of his house, and all that he had he put under his authority. So it was, from the time that he had made him overseer of his house and all that he had, that the LORD blessed the Egyptian's house for Joseph's sake; and the blessing of the LORD was on all that he had in the house and in the field. Thus he left all that he had in Joseph's hand, and he did not know what he had except for the bread which he ate.

Now Joseph was handsome in form and appearance. And it came to pass after these things that his master's wife cast longing eyes on Joseph, and she said, "Lie with me." But he refused and said to his master's wife, "Look, my master does not know what is with me in the house, and he has committed all that he has to my hand. There is no one greater in this house than I, nor has he kept back anything from me but you, because you are his wife. How then can I do this great wickedness, and sin against God?"

So it was, as she spoke to Joseph day by day, that he did not heed her, to lie with her or to be with her. But it happened about this time, when Joseph went into the house to do his work, and none of the men of the house was inside, that she caught him by his garment, saying, "Lie with me." But he left his garment in her hand, and fled and ran outside.

Genesis 39:1–12

In Genesis 39, God has taken wonderful principles for dealing with temptation and clothed them for us in a flesh and blood example in this man named Joseph. Probably between seventeen and twenty years old at the time, Joseph was an extremely attractive young man (verse 6). We also know from Genesis 37 that he was a man to whom God had given great dreams and for whom God had extraordinary plans. Joseph had been sold into slavery by his brothers, and he was the chief servant in Potiphar's house.

Potiphar's wife was after Joseph. And we can assume from Joseph's response to her repeated advances that she was without doubt very beautiful and represented a considerable temptation for him. As she actively tried to seduce Joseph—making her desires known to him, making herself available to him, boldly inviting him to lie with her, and when all else failed, grabbing his robe—what did Joseph do? He abandoned that robe and fled.

Now, stop and think about the power of that kind of temptation to a seventeen-year-old man who is a long, long way from home. Those of you who are seventeen know the power of that temptation. It is about as strong a temptation as there is in life. The so-called "experts" who study such things say that the male sexual desire is greatest between the ages of seventeen and twenty.

Now, you may be thinking, "What is this, a book on human sexuality? I'm not sure that I want to know all this! What's the point you are trying to make?" The point is Joseph is going *to stand and not succumb* in the area of his greatest temptation. In doing so, he gives each of us instruction on how *to stand* in the area of our greatest temptation — *even if our area of greatest temptation is entirely different from his.* So what did Joseph do in order to stand? He took six practical steps in the face of the strongest of temptations.

TEMPTATION

SELAH

Create in me a clean heart, O God, and renew a steadfast spirit within me.

Psalm 51:10

Out of the abundance of the heart the mouth speaks. A good man out of the good treasure of his heart brings forth good things, and an evil man out of the evil treasure brings forth evil things.

Matthew 12:34–35

For the word of God is living and powerful, and sharper than any two-edged sword, piercing even to the division of the soul and spirit, and of joints and marrow, and is a discerner of the thoughts and intents of the heart.

Hebrews 4:12

TEMPTATION

FOR FURTHER STUDY

Proverbs 4:23; Proverbs 16:18; Jeremiah 17:9; Matthew 15:19-20

Chapter Two

LIVE FAR FROM THE EDGE

The first step Joseph took was that he did not live near *the cliff edge* of sin. Genesis 39:10 says, "So it was, as she spoke to Joseph day by day, that he did not heed her, to lie with her ***or to be with her***" (emphasis mine). Joseph purposely structured his life so that he did not needlessly put himself near temptation. He created as much distance as possible between himself and the opportunity to sin. This was extremely wise because the day was coming when he would be going about his business as a slave and—bam!—right out of the blue, the boss' wife is grabbing his cloak and pulling him down on her.

Had Joseph been *living on the edge of the cliff* spiritually, the force of that temptation could very well have taken him over the edge! Have you noticed that you don't have to go out looking for temptation, but that temptation will come looking for you? Joseph understood this and worked hard to protect himself.

> *Have you noticed that you don't have to go out looking for temptation, but that temptation will come looking for you?*

Very often as Christians, we have a tendency to drift toward *the edge of the cliff*, especially in the areas of our greatest weaknesses. As new Christians, we can be so careful to distance ourselves from the old ways of sin that once dominated our lives. But after we have walked with the Lord for a while a crazy thing can happen—we can convince ourselves that we have reached a level of spiritual maturity that no longer requires us to *be as careful as we once were.* Before we know it, we are living closer to temptation than we would ever have allowed ourselves to live when we first came to the Lord. Pride has crept in and blinded us to impending danger. As Solomon wrote, "Pride goes before destruction, and a haughty spirit before a fall" (Proverbs 16:18).

When that *wind of temptation* comes down upon us—if we are *living on the edge*—there is nothing to hold on to, so *we go right over the cliff* into sin. The people who stand are the ones who walk like Joseph—as far away from that edge as possible. They're still going to be hit with temptation, but they will be in a safer place when it comes. Satan is a destroyer. That's all he knows. So he doesn't regard those weak little fences we build right on the edge. He just lulls us to sleep right there, knowing that the day is coming when he's going to blast us in that place.

In Psalm 18 King David wrote of the blessing of being in "a broad place" at the time of attack by a "strong enemy." Speaking of the Lord, David said, "He delivered me from my strong enemy, from those who hated me, for they were too strong for me. They confronted me in the day of my calamity, but the Lord was my support. He also brought me out into *a broad place*" (Psalm 18:17–19, emphasis mine). A broad place was an open space that provided a safe distance from the enemy's ambushes and traps. When that strong wind of temptation comes, it needs to find us in a broad place, far from the opportunity to sin.

Several decades ago, Billy Graham was in Modesto, California, where he and his associates established what they called *The Modesto Manifesto.* Part of that manifesto was a commitment never to travel alone, but instead to travel in pairs so that each man would remain above reproach, thereby keeping one another accountable as they sought to resist the temptations that came their way.

The Billy Graham team recognized the wisdom in following Jesus' model of sending disciples out by twos (Luke 10:1). Was that legalism on their part? No, that was wisdom on their part—wisdom to *stay away from the edge*, wisdom to put a safe distance between themselves and the opportunity to sin.

The Apostle Paul wrote, "Do you not know that those who run in a race all run, but one receives the prize? Run in such a way that you may obtain it. And everyone who competes for the prize is temperate in all things. Now they do it to obtain a perishable crown, but we for an imperishable crown. Therefore I run thus: not with uncertainty. Thus I fight: not as one who beats the air. But I discipline my body and bring it into subjection, lest, when I have preached to others, I myself should become disqualified" (I Corinthians 9:24–27).

Paul treated God's call upon his life as a priceless treasure. Thus, he was careful to guard it by deliberately structuring his life in such a way that he did not needlessly put himself near those things that aroused his sinful desires. Diligently protecting God's call upon our lives is critical because so much can hang in the balance that is beyond our awareness. God was going to use Joseph to impact the entire population of Egypt and to preserve the Hebrew people by bringing them through seven years of famine. The fate of two nations *hung in the balance* as the enemy tried to lure Joseph into the trap of adultery. We must do whatever is necessary to guard the dreams and visions God has given us, no matter what anybody else thinks, no matter how fanatical they might look to them.

THOUGHTS FOR APPLICATION

1. Has there been a time in my Christian life when I pursued holiness more than I do now?

2. Is the distance increasing or decreasing between what I know to be true from God's Word and the way I actually live?

3. Am I living too close to temptation? If so, what immediate changes do I need to make in my life to move into a broad, safe place instead of living near the edge of the cliff spiritually?

SELAH

A highway shall be there, and a road, and it shall be called the Highway of Holiness. The unclean shall not pass over it, but it shall be for others. Whoever walks the road, although a fool, shall not go astray.

Isaiah 35:8

My brethren, count it all joy when you fall into various trials, knowing that the testing of your faith produces patience. But let patience have its perfect work, that you may be perfect and complete, lacking nothing.

James 1:2–4

Therefore gird up the loins of your mind, be sober, and rest your hope fully upon the grace that is to be brought to you at the revelation of Jesus Christ; as obedient children, not conforming yourselves to the former lusts, as in your ignorance; but as He who called you is holy, you also be holy in all your conduct, because it is written, "Be holy, for I am holy."

I Peter 1:13–16

TEMPTATION
FOR FURTHER STUDY

Psalm 96:9; Romans 6:15–22; II Corinthians 6:17–7:1; Colossians 1:19–23; Hebrews 12:1–3; Hebrews 12:12–14; I John 3:2–3

Chapter Three

LEARN TO SAY "NO"

The second step Joseph took was to say, "No" to temptation. Genesis 39:8 says, "But *he refused* and said to his master's wife, 'Look, my master does not know what is with me in the house, and he has committed all that he has to my hand.'" It almost seems silly to ascribe nobility to something as simple as saying "No" to sin until one stops to realize how few people today are practiced in the art of saying "No" to anything at all. The idea that I ought to deny the sinful desires of my flesh, or even that I *can* deny them is increasingly a foreign concept. So often we're like Cocker Spaniel puppies. We roll right over and reveal our soft underbelly: "Satan, don't take too big of a bite." Instead, we should let the fact that we have the ability to say "No" to sin wash over us, replacing every bit of doubt and every thought of defeat with a bold faith and an absolute confidence of victory in the face of temptation.

You can say "No" to sin! Shout it from the mountaintops! I think it would be good to repeat it over and over until every argument and every high thing that exalts itself against what we know to be true about God is cast down (II Corinthians 10:3–5). The Spirit of God declared through James, "Therefore submit to God. *Resist* the devil and he will flee from you" (James 4:7, emphasis mine). But where does one start a life of resisting the temptation to do wrong? Some of you might need to look in the mirror in the morning and just practice saying "No" to yourselves in preparation for the day. "No, no, no, no . . . !" As you do, you might even feel a sense of faith and power surge inside of you. Like hitting an opponent with a body shot in boxing, every time you say "No" to the flesh, it loses a little steam. At first, it seems as if the body shots are doing little good, as if they are a waste of time—but over the long haul of the match, they take a tremendous toll on the opponent. Likewise, every time we say "No" to our flesh, it is weakened and beaten further into subjection.

Years ago, I heard an illustration that has always been helpful to me regarding the spiritual battle we face every day. As Christians, each of us has two natures: an old man and a new man. The new man is who and what I am because of the Holy Spirit living in me. The old man is the flesh, the person I used to be before becoming a Christian. One day when we pass from this life into eternity, we will be rid of the old nature, and the battle with the flesh will finally be over. In the meantime, the old man wants to fight the Holy Spirit for control of our lives. We are to cooperate with Him in making sure that doesn't happen.

How? Imagine you are out walking two very large dogs down the street, one white and one black. Let's say the white dog represents the new nature and the black dog represents the old nature. Each dog will want to pull you in a completely opposite direction. Which dog will exert the greater pull and influence? The one you feed. If you feed the white dog and starve the black dog, the white dog will have the greater influence. Conversely, if you feed the black dog and starve the white dog, the black dog will have the strength to pull you in the direction it wants to go. You feed the spirit and starve the flesh every time you are confronted with temptation and you say, "Yes" to what God says you should do in the situation and "No" to what your flesh wants to do. Joseph said "No" to his flesh and "Yes" to God in every encounter with Potiphar's wife. In doing so he walked in victory, making no provision for the flesh (Romans 13:14).

I have a friend who lives one of the most Christ-like lives I have ever seen. To look at him you might think that he hardly deals with temptation at all. One day I heard him say, "The life of holiness means saying 'No' to the flesh ten thousand times a day." Like Joseph, my friend models a key to holy living. Saying "No" to sinful desires must become a life-defining habit for those who want to live a holy life.

"The life of holiness means saying 'No' to the flesh ten thousand times a day."

Joseph shows us that we can fend off even the strongest of temptations. But notice that Joseph didn't simply say "No" to temptation; he said "No" for good reasons.

THOUGHTS FOR APPLICATION

1. In what areas of my life do I regularly say, "No" to my fleshly desires in order to say, "Yes" to God's commandments?

2. Is spiritual discipline and the denial of self a part of my daily life?

3. If I am not in the habit of saying, "No" to my flesh, in what small area can I start to develop this habit so I can begin to train myself to know what it feels like? (For example: stopping at stop signs, driving the speed limit, only eating until I am full, getting up or going to sleep at a certain time of the day or night, clearing the table after dinner for the family, etc.)

4. Which nature do I feed: the old or the new?

5. What portion of my life goes into feeding my flesh versus feeding the spirit? Practically speaking, what radio stations or music do I listen to, what movies do I watch, how much television—versus how much time I spend in church attendance, Bible study, worship, service to the Lord, etc.?

TEMPTATION
SELAH

Turn away my eyes from looking at worthless things, and revive me in Your way.

Psalm 119:37

Then Jesus said to His disciples, "If anyone desires to come after Me, let him deny himself, and take up his cross, and follow Me. For whoever desires to save his life will lose it, but whoever loses his life for My sake will find it."

Matthew 16:24–25

Finally, brethren, whatever things are true, whatever things are noble, whatever things are just, whatever things are pure, whatever things are lovely, whatever things are of good report, if there is any virtue and if there is anything praiseworthy—meditate on these things.

Philippians 4:8

TEMPTATION
FOR FURTHER STUDY

Matthew 26:41; Romans 8:1–17; Romans 12:1–2; I Corinthians 9:24–27; Galatians 5:16–25; Ephesians 2:1–5; Colossians 3:1–11; I Peter 5:8–9

Chapter Four

CONSIDER THE CONSEQUENCES AHEAD OF TIME

The third lesson we learn from Joseph is that he was successful because he had considered the consequences of sin ahead of time. Genesis 39:8–9 says, "But he refused and said to his master's wife, 'Look, *my master* does not know what is with me in the house, and *he* has committed all that *he* has to my hand. There is no one greater in this house than I, nor has *he* kept back anything from me but you, because you are *his wife*. How then can I do this great wickedness, and *sin against God?*'"

Essentially, Joseph told Potiphar's wife, "Your husband has been more than generous to me. How could I betray him like this?!" Joseph realized how far-reaching the consequences of his sin would be, that it wouldn't just affect the two of them but would greatly impact others as well. His decisive rebuke tells me that Joseph had thought through the consequences of this sin ahead of time. It is essential that we also think through the far-reaching consequences of sin before we begin going down the path that leads to sin. It is so critical to count the cost in advance and ask ourselves, "Is it worth it?"

It is so critical to count the cost in advance and ask ourselves, "Is it worth it?"

I have known "Christian" men through the years who have left their wives and children for other women and after one week would have given their right arms to have them back. In many cases, it was too late. These men didn't think through the consequences of their sin before they took that first step toward sin.

It is critical for all of us to sit down and give long, sober thought to the repercussions of giving in to sin. To ask ourselves, "What will this do to my faithful wife? What will this do to my hardworking husband? What will this do to my children, to their innocent lives? What will this do to my grandchildren?" As pastors and church leaders, we need to ask, "What destruction will this sow into the lives of the precious saints who attend the church?" The whole world is shaking around them, and they like to think that no matter how bad it gets in the world at least their church is a strong, stable refuge. One act of foolish selfishness can shower disillusionment and discouragement upon them. Christian leaders, indeed all of us, need to ask, "What effect would this sin have upon the city God has called me to minister in, upon the name of Christ?" Joseph considered what he would be throwing away if he gave in to sin. He considered how it would affect others. Then he asked himself, "Is it really worth it?" and wisely decided it was not.

As I read this account from Joseph's life, I get the distinct impression that he did not wait until he was *in the middle* of that temptation to figure out what he would do. It seems that in his heart he had settled the issue of how he would react if he ever faced such a temptation long before the opportunity ever came along. This is critical. If a man finds himself in the situation Joseph was in and *only then* begins to try and figure out what he ought to do, *that man is in deep trouble!* We need to determine exactly how we will respond long before temptation ever comes knocking on our door.

THOUGHTS FOR APPLICATION

1. What is the area of my greatest temptation?

2. What will be the consequences if I give in to that temptation? To my relationship with the Lord, to my wife or husband, children, grandchildren, parents, my church, to God's reputation?

3. Is it really worth it?

TEMPTATION
SELAH

The heart is deceitful above all things, and desperately wicked; who can know it? I, the LORD, search the heart, I test the mind, even to give every man according to his ways, according to the fruit of his doings.

Jeremiah 17:9–10

Do not be deceived, God is not mocked; for whatever a man sows, that he will also reap. For he who sows to his flesh will of the flesh reap corruption, but he who sows to the Spirit will of the Spirit reap everlasting life.

Galatians 6:7–8

If we confess our sins, He is faithful and just to forgive us our sins and to cleanse us from all unrighteousness.

I John 1:9

TEMPTATION
FOR FURTHER STUDY

Proverbs 6:26–29; Romans 8:6; I Thessalonians 4:3–8; James 1:15–16

Chapter Five

LEAD US NOT INTO TEMPTATION

Jesus recognized our need to be prepared every morning before we head out into a new day of "ten thousand 'No's'." He taught us to pray daily, "And do not lead us into temptation, but deliver us from the evil one" (Luke 11:4b). Why does He want us to pray that prayer every day? Because He knows we are going to be tempted to sin every day. He wants us to begin each day with a fresh sensitivity to the coming spiritual warfare so that *when* it occurs we will not be surprised by it, but rather we will be anticipating it.

Taking time to pray not only infuses us with spiritual power, but it gives us an opportunity to commit our thoughts, our emotions, and our wills to God and to establish a battle plan. So that, like Joseph, when temptation comes our way, we can say to it, "Oh, good morning, I've been expecting you. God and I have already been talking about you today. In fact, I have been practicing for this moment. No!!!!!!!!" It is so important to settle the issue of what we are going to do before we find ourselves suddenly in the middle of tempting situations. We can pray, "Oh Lord, keep us from places of needless temptation. Let the opportunity to sin not coincide with the desire to sin." That is the prayer of one who, like Joseph, possesses a necessary vigilance regarding temptation.

Perhaps your Christian life is one of almost unbroken defeat and failure. When was the last time you started your day talking specifically with Him about it as a part of your devotional life? How often we can go days, weeks, and months, in the midst of the most severe spiritual warfare, and fail to cry out even once, "Lord, lead me not into temptation, but deliver me from evil." Let's make that cry a part of our morning prayer, for surely any prayer He has modeled is a prayer He will always be completely faithful to answer.

THOUGHTS FOR APPLICATION

1. Do I follow Jesus' instruction by having a time of daily Bible reading and prayer that includes preparation for the temptations that will come my way?

2. What is my battle plan for overcoming temptations I face on a daily basis?

3. Do I believe Jesus will answer my prayer to be delivered from temptation?

TEMPTATION
SELAH

And he did evil, because he did not prepare his heart to seek the LORD.

II Chronicles 12:14

And do not present your members as instruments of unrighteousness to sin, but present yourselves to God as being alive from the dead, and your members as instruments of righteousness to God. For sin shall not have dominion over you, for you are not under law but under grace.

Romans 6:13–14

Now to Him who is able to do exceedingly abundantly above all that we ask or think, according to the power that works in us, to Him be glory in the church by Christ Jesus to all generations, forever and ever. Amen.

Ephesians 3:20–21

TEMPTATION
FOR FURTHER STUDY

Psalm 119:9–11; Proverbs 6:20–24; Matthew 26:41; Ephesians 6:10–17; Philippians 4:13

Chapter Six

SEE SIN AS "GREAT WICKEDNESS"

The fourth Biblical truth we learn from Joseph is that he considered sin to be *great wickedness*. He said, "How then can I do this great wickedness, and sin against God?" (Genesis 39:9) As I read this passage, I am struck by the strength of the words he chooses: "great wickedness." When was the last time you heard the world call pleasure "wicked"? When was the last time you heard the word "wicked" ascribed to even the vilest acts?

Some time ago I was watching the news on television when it was reported that a man in Australia had taken a rifle and opened fire on a large crowd of people, killing many. Clearly shaken by the events, the news reporter declared, "A great evil has visited our country today." As I listened, the word "evil" hit me like a ton of bricks. I thought to myself, "When was the last time I heard the press, or any secular institution, refer to anything as 'evil'?" Like "wickedness," "evil" is a word that is hardly used anymore because very little is thought to be evil.

As Christians, are we appalled by sin?

But enough about the failure of the world to be appalled by sin; as Christians, are we appalled by sin? Joseph was appalled at what Potiphar's wife was proposing and it was a critical part of what protected him from sin. When was the last time we used the word "evil" or "wickedness" in reference to the sins that tempt us? Even though the world has ceased by and large to use the word "wickedness" in reference to personal morality, as Christians we had better keep it alive in our vocabularies. I think of how much of the entertainment industry — movies, television, music, etc. — that lures us today would have been immediately assessed by Joseph as "great wickedness." Yet, we as Christians watch and listen without the slightest conviction that we are doing anything wrong, much less that it is abhorrent. *We need to put away anything and everything from our lives that would cause us to stop seeing what God calls "wickedness" as just that, wickedness.*

The Psalmist declared, "You who love the Lord, *hate* evil!" (Psalm 97:10, emphasis mine). To the Romans the Apostle Paul wrote, "*Abhor* what is evil. Cling to what is good" (Romans 12:9, emphasis mine). There is a holy zeal revealed in the strength of those words, isn't there? We need that zeal. As bold as the world becomes in its wickedness, we must be equally zealous for holiness. The Holy Spirit uses the phrase "the beauty of holiness" four times in the Bible. A holy life is a beautiful life in God's sight. Purity and innocence are precious to Him and must be fervently protected if they are to characterize our lives.

THOUGHTS FOR APPLICATION

1. What is my attitude toward sin? Do I abhor evil as God directs that I should?

2. What do I consider to be wicked? Do I use the words "evil" or "wicked" to describe the sins that tempt me?

3. Am I still shocked by wickedness? If not, where am I getting my definitions of right and wrong, good and bad, pure and impure?

4. Have I become conformed to this world or is there a distinctiveness to my life that sets me apart from the world around me? Am I salt and light?

5. Has my thinking been fashioned after this world?

TEMPTATION
SELAH

I will set nothing wicked before my eyes; I hate the work of those who fall away; it shall not cling to me. A perverse heart shall depart from me; I will not know wickedness.

Psalm 101:3–4

If then you were raised with Christ, seek those things which are above, where Christ is, sitting at the right hand of God. Set your mind on things above, not on things on the earth. For you died, and your life is hidden with Christ in God.

Colossians 3:1–3

Test all things; hold fast what is good. Abstain from every form of evil.

I Thessalonians 5:21–22

TEMPTATION
FOR FURTHER STUDY

Romans 8:5; Romans 12:1–2; I Peter 4:1–4; I John 1:5–7; I John 2:15–17

Chapter Seven

LOVING GOD MORE THAN SIN

The fifth lesson we learn from Joseph is that he realized to do this "great wickedness" would be to wrong God. In verse 9, he declares, "How then can I do this great wickedness, and sin against God?" (Genesis 39:9) Joseph understood that committing this act would not only be a sin against Potiphar, but that it would be an even greater sin against God. He was saying, "This would not be right to do to Him — He has been so good and gracious to me; I couldn't bear to hurt Him or wound His great heart." This tells me that Joseph's relationship with the Lord meant more to him than what sin had to offer.

A close, personal relationship with Jesus is the single greatest safeguard against sin.

It also tells me that Joseph was *current* in his personal relationship with God. Someone has said, "It takes a passion to conquer a passion." It's true, isn't it? The key isn't to hate sin more, but to love Jesus more. A close, personal relationship with Jesus is the single greatest safeguard against sin because it is much harder to sin against a precious and valued relationship than it is to sin against rules. The hardest thing in the world to sin against is love. Yes, by all means let's get rid of the junk in our lives, but then let's grow in our love for Jesus until our relationship with Him means more to us than anything sin and this world have to offer.

THOUGHTS FOR APPLICATION

1. Do I hate the thought of hurting the heart of God?

2. Have I considered what it cost God to pay for my sin?

3. Do I consider how it will grieve the Holy Spirit who lives inside me if I give in to sin?

4. Do I really love God more than the sinful pleasures of this world?

TEMPTATION
SELAH

Many waters cannot quench love, nor can the floods drown it. If a man would give for love all the wealth of his house, it would be utterly despised.

Song of Solomon 8:7

Jesus answered them, "Most assuredly, I say to you, whoever commits sin is a slave of sin. And a slave does not abide in the house forever, but a son abides forever. Therefore if the Son makes you free, you shall be free indeed."

John 8:34–36

And He said to me, "It is done! I am the Alpha and the Omega, the Beginning and the End. I will give of the fountain of the water of life freely to him who thirsts. He who overcomes shall inherit all things, and I will be his God and he shall be My son."

Revelation 21:6–7

TEMPTATION
FOR FURTHER STUDY

I Corinthians 6:12–20; Ephesians 3:16–19; I Peter 1:3–9; I John 4:17–21; Revelation 2:4–5

Chapter Eight

RUN!

The sixth Biblical truth we learn from Joseph is that there can be times in our lives when a temptation is so strong that we will need to physically *run* from it in order to survive. If a man as spiritual as Joseph found it necessary to run from sin, then we can be sure that the day may well be coming in our lives when the only way out of a temptation will be to leave everything behind and run. Why? Because in the midst of strong temptation, especially in the area of our greatest weakness, there is a line that, if crossed, will largely break down our resistance to sin. We move from being under the control of the Holy Spirit to being under the control of our sinful desires, and those desires will run headlong into sin until they have satisfied themselves. We are then left in shame and with crushing condemnation—knowing all we can do is repent, confess our sin to God, and ask His forgiveness. Then come the consequences—to us, to the innocent, to the name of Christ. Thus, we must do whatever is necessary to keep ourselves from going over that line.

When I was a new Christian, I heard a tape series by a man named Bob Vernon. Produced by the "Firefighters for Christ" organization, it was called "The True Masculine Role." Bob Vernon gave an illustration that has stayed with me through the years in which he likened temptation to buying a coke from a vending machine. He put it something like this: Let's say you go to a coke machine and it says, "Coke $1.00. Insert four quarters." You have four quarters in your hand so you put the first quarter into the machine. At that point, you still have control over whether a coke is going to come down that chute or not because you can still hit the "coin return" lever to stop the transaction. You put in the second quarter and you still have control. So it is after you insert the third quarter. But after you insert that fourth quarter, to save your life, you cannot keep that coke from coming down the chute.

It's the same with temptation. We need to do *whatever it takes* to make sure that we are never standing in front of that coke machine with four quarters in our hand, much less with three quarters already inserted. Sin, especially life-dominating sin, typically establishes a pattern in a person's life. A person will engage in that life-dominating sin at certain physical locations, at certain times of the day or night, and around certain people. The pattern needs to be broken. The key is to take those four quarters and make sure we never have them all together in our pocket at the same time. Drop one from the Golden Gate Bridge, throw another into the back seat of a car going to Kansas, drop another one down a storm drain in New York City, and give the final quarter as a tip to a mime in Paris—so that *to save your life,* you cannot bring those four quarters together to put them into the machine. That kind of aggressive action is what is necessary to win the battle against temptation.

The ruthlessness of sin requires ruthlessness with sin.

We need to make sure that we never find ourselves in that place, at that time, with those people, exposed to those things. Why? Because the ruthlessness *of* sin requires ruthlessness *with* sin. Remember, James told us, "When desire has conceived, it gives birth to sin, and *sin when it is full-grown brings forth death. Do not be deceived,* my beloved brethren" (James 1:15–16, emphasis mine). Sin will never be content merely to bring us into a life of defeat and condemnation—it is more ruthless than even that; it is always working to destroy us and our fellowship with God.

The Bible declares, "No temptation has overtaken you except such as is common to man; but God is faithful, who will not allow you to be tempted beyond what you are able, but with the temptation will also make a way of escape, that you may be able to bear it" (I Corinthians 10:13). The Apostle Paul wrote to Timothy, "*Flee* youthful lusts" (II Timothy 2:22, emphasis mine). Perhaps he was thinking of Joseph when he wrote those words. Both Joseph and Paul realized that flight is sometimes necessary to protect ourselves from sin. But the flight to safety must always take place while we are still under the control of the Holy Spirit, before that line is crossed.

THOUGHTS FOR APPLICATION

1. What is my typical pattern for giving in to the sins I struggle with?

2. What do I need to do to break that cycle? What specific people, places, or things do I need to turn away from in order to succeed?

3. What steps do I need to take to make sure that the desire for sin doesn't ever coincide with the opportunity to sin?

TEMPTATION
SELAH

But my eyes are upon You, O GOD the Lord; in You I take refuge; do not leave my soul destitute. Keep me from the snares they have laid for me, and from the traps of the workers of iniquity. Let the wicked fall into their own nets, while I escape safely.

Psalm 141:8–10

The name of the LORD is a strong tower; the righteous run to it and are safe.

Proverbs 18:10

Flee also youthful lusts; but pursue righteousness, faith, love, peace with those who call on the Lord out of a pure heart.

II Timothy 2:22

TEMPTATION
FOR FURTHER STUDY

Psalm 68:20; Psalm 71:1–3; Proverbs 4:12; II Peter 2:9

Chapter Nine

THE "HOW" OF RESISTING TEMPTATION

Well, there you have it, *what* we are to do in the face of temptation from the life of Joseph. I could wrap things up by declaring, "There you have the *what* God's Word says, now go and do it." And for some that would be an adequate conclusion. They might even think, "That is a fine study on a needed subject." But there are others who might be left more frustrated than ever. Their frustration would express itself in a single word, "How?" They would cry out with the Apostle Paul from the book of Romans, "For to will is present with me, but *how* to perform what is good I do not find" (Romans 7:18b, emphasis mine). Paul is saying, "I know *what* I am supposed to do, that is not my problem. I want to live a holy life but my problem is with the *how*—I lack the necessary power." So let me conclude by addressing the "how" of the Holy Spirit that is always behind the "what" of God's Word.

Several years ago, a friend of mine came to visit me. Over breakfast, he expressed that he was having difficulty finding a church to attend in his community. I knew there were many churches in his area so, trying to understand, I asked, "What are you running into?" He told me a story that he said was typical of his experience.

My friend had attended a Sunday morning service at a church of about four hundred people. As the pastor delivered his sermon, he revealed details of a counseling appointment from earlier in the week as an illustration. A young woman in her mid-twenties had gotten pregnant as a teenager and her mother had virtually forced her to have an abortion. During the procedure, things not only went tragically wrong for the baby, but also for her. She ended up sterilized as a result, unable to ever have children again. Now years later, as a Christian, she was struggling not only from guilt over her sin, but also with tremendous bitterness and hatred toward her mother. She was especially distressed over the fact that she'd never be able to have the one thing she wanted—children of her own.

My friend sat in that congregation, amazed that the pastor would reveal such an intensely private situation in the course of a sermon. He wondered how the preacher was going to tie this whole thing together, and seal up the can of worms he had opened. He didn't have to wait long to find out. The pastor said, "You know what I told this woman in the counseling appointment? I told her that she just had to forgive her mom."

My friend was outraged. He said, "I almost jumped out of the pew." The pastor made no mention of God providing her with the power to forgive, no mention of forgiving her mother in response to the tremendous forgiveness God had shown her, no mention of forgiving her mother in order to be a witness of God's forgiveness in the situation. I insisted that he was mistaken—surely, the pastor had explained to the young woman not only her responsibility to forgive but also the *why* and *how* behind God's command. He said, "No, that's exactly the way it was."

What was his great frustration? Was this pastor wrong in what he had said? No, what he said was absolutely correct as far as he went. The problem was that he didn't go far enough. Thus the woman and the congregation were left with the idea that we are to live this Christian life in the strength of our own flesh, that God has revealed His will in the Bible and now it is up to us to roll up our sleeves and obey it. This is a tragically incomplete perception of Christianity that can produce very, very frustrated and condemned Christians.

Jon Courson has well said, "Christianity is not the imitation of Jesus in the power of our flesh, but rather the impartation of the Holy Spirit." It is not, "Okay, here's what God says in His Word, now let's obey it by sheer willpower." It is the empowering of the Holy Spirit.

> *"Christianity is not the imitation of Jesus in the power of our flesh, but rather the impartation of the Holy Spirit."*

Suppose I travel to San Francisco and come across a master artist creating a painting of the Golden Gate Bridge and the beauty of the bay surrounding it. As I watch him paint with such skill and beauty, I think to myself that I would like to paint such a painting too. So I ask the artist where he got his canvas, his easel, his brushes, and his paints, then I race to the store to purchase the necessary supplies. Within the hour I have my easel set up next to his and I begin to paint that same scene, imitating his every move, matching his every stroke, changing brushes when he does, dipping into the same colors he does.

At the end of the day a crowd gathers "oohing" and "ahhing" over the tremendous beauty he has captured on his canvas, while my best attempt inspires only snickers and pity. As I sit down frustrated and condemned wondering what it would take for me to be able to paint like him, suddenly it dawns on me that the only way for me to paint a painting with his skill and beauty would be if he somehow took up residence within me and painted it through me.

That is Christianity, the Spirit of God coming into me to live the life of Jesus through me, providing me not only with the will to do what pleases God but the power as well. This is what Paul described in writing to the Christians at Philippi, "For it is God who works *in* you both to will and to do for His good pleasure" (Philippians 2:13, emphasis mine).

Now we have not only the "what" of God's Word but also the "how" of God's Holy Spirit. Why can I have victory over temptation as a Christian? Because God Almighty in the person of the Holy Spirit indwells me and gives me both the desire and the power to obey His Word. He is the "how" behind the "what" of God's Word.

This Christian life is a supernatural life that can only be lived through the supernatural power that He eagerly gives. Jesus declared, "But you shall *receive power* when the Holy Spirit has come upon you; and *you shall be witnesses* to Me in Jerusalem, and in all Judea and Samaria, and to the end of the earth" (Acts 1: 8, emphasis mine). Luke 11:13 says, "If you then, being evil, know how to give good gifts to your children, how much more will your heavenly Father give the Holy Spirit *to those who ask* Him!" With a sincere heart and childlike faith, simply ask Him for the power to live a life like Jesus and He will give it to you. No Christian is ever the same person after having prayed that prayer. Jesus, our Savior, our Lord, and our Friend, is not only eager for us to *know* all the glorious truth revealed in the Scriptures, but He also desires that we fully *experience* those truths. He will be faithful to personally take us by the hand and walk us into all the fullness and beauty of the life He has prepared for us. "He who calls you is faithful, *who also will do it*" (I Thessalonians 5:24, emphasis mine).

THOUGHTS FOR APPLICATION

1. Is the Spirit-empowered life a reality for me?

2. If not, am I willing to believe, in faith, that the Holy Spirit will empower me to live the Christian life and then am I willing to begin walking in that power?

TEMPTATION
SELAH

For God has not given us a spirit of fear, but of power and of love and of a sound mind.

II Timothy 1:7

For we do not have a High Priest who cannot sympathize with our weaknesses, but was in all points tempted as we are, yet without sin. Let us therefore come boldly to the throne of grace, that we may obtain mercy and find grace to help in time of need.

Hebrews 4:15–16

His divine power has given to us all things that pertain to life and godliness, through the knowledge of Him who called us by glory and virtue, by which have been given to us exceedingly great and precious promises, that through these you may be partakers of the divine nature, having escaped the corruption that is in the world through lust.

II Peter 1:3–4

TEMPTATION
FOR FURTHER STUDY

II Corinthians 4:7; Colossians 2:10; Hebrews 2:16–18; I Peter 1:3–5

THE SIX STEPS

Let's review the six lessons we learn from Joseph for successfully standing in the face of temptation:

First, Joseph teaches us the importance of not living near the cliff edge of sin—of purposely structuring our lives so that we create as much distance from temptation as possible. We will still be tempted but we will be in a safe place when it happens.

Second, Joseph teaches us that we can say "No" to even the strongest of temptations. Like a body shot in boxing, every time we say "No" the flesh loses a little steam.

Third, Joseph teaches us the importance of considering the consequences of sin ahead of time. Is the momentary pleasure of sin really worth it?

Fourth, Joseph teaches us the importance of seeing sin as "great wickedness." He didn't have a casual attitude towards sin.

Fifth, Joseph teaches us the importance of having a relationship with God which means more to us than anything sin has to offer. Love is a greater motivator for holy living than rules will ever be.

Sixth, Joseph teaches us that flight is sometimes necessary to protect ourselves from sin. But, the flight to safety must always take place while we are still under the control of the Holy Spirit, before that line of broken resistance is crossed.

Just as these Biblical truths worked to enable Joseph to successfully stand in the area of his greatest temptation, so they will help you to stand in the areas of your greatest temptations—even if they are different from his. God had tremendous plans for Joseph's life, far beyond his wildest dreams, just as God has tremendous plans for your life. There will be temptations between now and the full revelation of those plans. Until then, may you be both wise and ruthless in your battle with temptation by the power of God's Holy Spirit.

THE MOST IMPORTANT STEP

Perhaps as you've read this book, a desire to be freed from the power of sin has been stirred within you. However, you've come to realize that you are not a Christian—God's Holy Spirit does not dwell within you. In order to say "No" to temptation, you must first say "Yes" to Christ. Entering into a personal relationship with Jesus is very simple.

1. The Bible teaches us that God loves us and wants to have a personal relationship with us.

   God is love.

   I John 4:8

   But God demonstrates His own love toward us, in that while we were still sinners, Christ died for us.

   Romans 5:8, emphasis mine

2. The "bad news" is that our sin has separated us from God and the relationship for which we were created.

For *all have sinned and fall short* of the glory of God. . . .

Romans 3:23, emphasis mine

3. But the "good news" is that God loved us so much that He sent His Son Jesus to pay the price we couldn't pay for the forgiveness of our sins.

    For God so loved the world that He gave His only begotten Son, that whoever believes in Him should not perish but have everlasting life.

    John 3:16–17, emphasis mine

You personally receive God's forgiveness and salvation by turning from your old sinful ways, trusting in Jesus' death upon the cross as the satisfying payment for the forgiveness of your sins, and surrendering your life to God to be used for His purposes. When you do this, God's Holy Spirit personally comes into your heart and begins to develop the character of Jesus *within* you and to live the life of Jesus *through* you. Jesus' life was the most attractive and blessed life ever lived on this earth. To enter into this relationship is to enter into life as God intends it for you. It is truly the greatest life imaginable.

If you would like to begin this personal relationship with God, you can do so right now by sincerely praying . . .

"Dear Lord Jesus, I confess that I am a sinner and that I have been less than perfect in my life. Thank You for dying on the cross for my sins. Right now, I turn from my old sinful ways, and I surrender my life to You. Please take control of it and make me into the person You want me to be. Thank You for forgiving my sins and giving me everlasting life. Amen."

If you prayed that prayer, the Bible declares that sin no longer has control over your life. Jesus said in John 8:36, "If the Son makes you free, you shall be free indeed." In order to walk in that freedom, you need to take some practical steps to grow strong spiritually: read the Bible, pray, and go to a Bible-teaching church to learn more about what it means to be a Christian. You can be confident that "He who has begun a good work in you will complete it until the day of Jesus Christ" (Philippians 1:6).

OTHER BOOKS BY DAMIAN KYLE

The Place of
Brokenness
in the Life of the Believer

1-931667-52-7

Our God is
a Blessing God

1-931667-60-8

OTHER MATERIALS AVAILABLE

Visit Calvary Chapel Modesto's website for additional audio messages by Pastor Damian Kyle. Access them by logging onto their website at:

www.calvarychapelmodesto.com

Audio tapes are also available by calling 209-545-5530, by writing to 4300 American Avenue, Modesto, California 95356, or by e-mailing:

tapelibrary@calvarychapelmodesto.com